CITIES
CAIRO

ABDO
Publishing Company

Nancy Furstinger

visit us at
www.abdopub.com

Published by ABDO Publishing Company, 4940 Viking Drive, Edina, Minnesota 55435.
Copyright © 2005 by Abdo Consulting Group, Inc. International copyrights reserved in all
countries. No part of this book may be reproduced in any form without written permission from
the publisher. The Checkerboard Library™ is a trademark and logo of ABDO Publishing Company.

Printed in the United States.

Cover Photo: Corbis
Interior Photos: Corbis pp. 1, 6-7, 10, 11, 13, 14, 15, 16, 17, 20, 21, 23, 26, 27, 29;
    Getty Images pp. 4, 5, 19, 25

Series Coordinator: Jennifer R. Krueger
Editors: Heidi M. Dahmes, Jennifer R. Krueger
Art Direction & Maps: Neil Klinepier

Library of Congress Cataloging-in-Publication Data

Furstinger, Nancy.
    Cairo / Nancy Furstinger.
       p. cm. -- (Cities)
    ISBN 1-59197-856-4
    1. Cairo (Egypt)--Juvenile literature. I. Title.

  DT143.F94 2005
  962'.16--dc22

                                                              2004046220

CONTENTS

CAIRO

The Great Sphinx is thought to have been made in the likeness of King Khafre, son of King Khufu. To Arabs, the Sphinx is known as Abu al-Hawl, which means "Father of Terror."

Cairo is the capital of Egypt and the largest city in Africa. It spreads out on the east and west banks of the Nile River. The desert surrounds the city on three sides.

Today, Cairo fuses past and present. Ancient buildings have been replaced by modern skyscrapers. The lights of modern Cairo shine on the ancient sites of a historic city.

These sites include the Great Sphinx and the Pyramids. Along the horizon, ancient mosques rise above the city's

A modern attraction in Cairo is the 607-foot (185-m) Cairo Tower. A revolving restaurant sits at the top of the tower. This landmark provides an excellent view of the city.

palm trees. In bazaars much like those in the 1300s, vendors still sell camels. And, unearthed treasures from King Tutankhamen's tomb are displayed in Cairo's Egyptian Museum.

Cairo has been growing and spreading since it was founded more than 1,000 years ago. The city's mounting population and modernization put its most famous sites at risk.

CAIRO AT A GLANCE

Date of Founding: **969**

Population: **16.5 million**

Metro Area: **83 square miles (215 sq km)**

Average Temperatures:

- **67° Fahrenheit (19 °C) in cold season**
- **95° Fahrenheit (35 °C) in warm season**

Annual Rainfall: **1 inch (3 cm)**

Elevation: **76 feet (23 m)**

Landmarks: **Pyramids of Giza, Great Sphinx**

Money: **Egyptian Pound**

Language: **Arabic**

FUN FACTS

The first McDonald's in Egypt opened in 1994. Seven years later, McDonald's introduced the McFalafel. The falafel is Egypt's favorite food. And, McDonald's wanted to be able to serve a "local sandwich with a local taste."

Al-Mansuriyah was Cairo's original name. It wasn't until 973–974 that the name Al-Qahirah, or Cairo, was given to the city.

TIMELINE

969 - The Fatimids conquer Egypt and build Cairo.

1953 - Egypt becomes a republic.

1956 - Gamal Abdel Nasser is elected the first president of Egypt.

1970 - The Aswan High Dam is completed.

1979 - Egypt signs a peace treaty with Israel.

1981 - Anwar el-Sadat is assassinated; Hosni Mubarak becomes president.

1987 - Cairo opens the first subway in Africa.

1999 - President Mubarak is elected to his fourth term.

THE VICTORIOUS

Several important ancient cities stood near where Cairo is today. The first king of Egypt, Menes, founded the capital of Memphis around 3100 BC. It was built near the head of the Nile River **delta**.

North of Memphis, the Romans occupied Babylon about 3,000 years later. In AD 641, 'Amr ibn al-'As founded Al-Fustat as a military camp.

Then in 969, Muslim **sect** members called Fatimids conquered Egypt. The Fatimids built their new city northeast of ancient Babylon and Al-Fustat. They called it *Al-Qahirah*, or *Cairo*, meaning "The Victorious." It has remained the capital of Egypt ever since.

Cairo expanded under the new rulers. In the late 1100s, Babylon and Al-Fustat became part of Cairo. During the 1300s, the city became the center of trade between Europe and the East.

Over the years, many people have ruled Egypt. In 1914, Britain assumed control of the country. But during **World War I**, an Egyptian movement for national freedom gained strength. The British failed to reach a settlement with the nationalists. And in 1922, Britain declared Egypt independent.

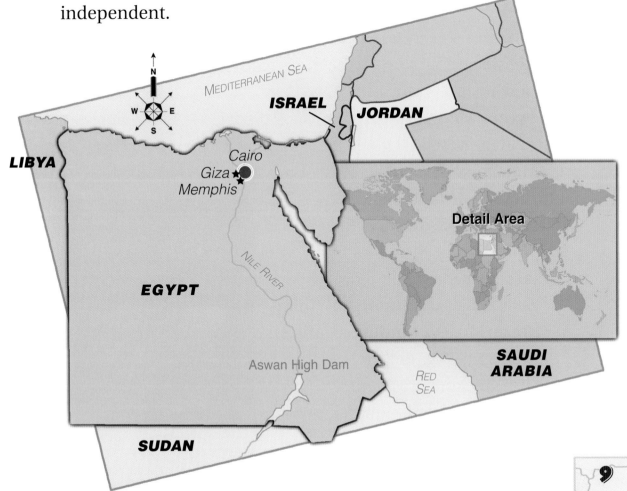

CAIRO'S LEADERS

In 1953, Egypt became a republic. At that time, citizens began electing a president. One of the most popular, Gamal Abdel Nasser, governed the country from 1956 until 1970. He was considered by some to be the greatest leader since the **pharaohs**.

Nasser was followed by Anwar el-Sadat. He launched the Arab-Israeli War in October 1973. Sadat began negotiating a peace treaty with Israel in 1978. Both he and Israeli prime minister Menachem Begin were awarded the Nobel Peace Prize for this work. Egypt and Israel finally signed a peace treaty in 1979.

Sadat was **assassinated** in Cairo in 1981 by Muslim **fundamentalists**. After the assassination, Hosni Mubarak became president. Egyptians re-elected Mubarak to his fourth term in 1999.

Hosni Mubarak

Egypt has 26 districts called governorates. Cairo is one of them. The president selects a governor to be the head of Cairo. Then, the city is divided into districts and villages, which are run by officials. Councils at each level of the local government aid the leaders.

BUSY STREETS

In the older parts of the city, donkey-drawn carts are still used. However, they are slowly vanishing. Today, overcrowded buses and minibuses are the most common forms of transportation. It is not uncommon to see passengers hanging on the outside of buses.

Cairo's growing population has caused many transportation problems. The city has built highways and overpasses to reduce traffic problems. However, driving is a dangerous sport in Cairo! Drivers often ignore road signs. But, police are enforcing new laws with harsh penalties.

Cairo does have good public transportation. In 1987, Cairo became home to the first subway in Africa. Many residents use this metropolitan rail system. To travel to other major cities, residents use the international airport and trains.

Opposite Page: To ensure safety on Cairo's streets, police issue tickets to people who drive at night without their lights on, run red lights, and excessively honk their horns.

ANCIENT CRAFTS

Cairo is the commercial center of Egypt. Cairo's major industry is **textile** making. The country's most important agricultural export is cotton. Factories also churn out cars, aircraft, food, iron, and steel. Tourism plays an important role in Cairo's **economy**, too.

Metal pots are among the many goods for sale at Cairo's various markets.

In workshops throughout the city, people still employ ancient skills. There are about 150,000 small, private workshops. Leather workers use camel skins for their creations. Hatmakers form red **fezzes** while coppersmiths hammer out designs. And, weavers create luxurious carpets.

Many of these crafts can be purchased in the Khan al-Khalili bazaar. This bazaar hosts hundreds of stalls. Some sell gold, brass, and cloth. Others sell spices and perfumes.

The sights, sounds, and smells of Cairo's markets haven't changed much since the 1300s. Camel caravans once crossed deserts carrying shoppers. Today, many bargain hunters come in tour buses. However, Egypt's largest camel market still exists outside of Cairo. Hundreds of camels are sold daily.

Camels are sold for farmwork or slaughter. They are also traded for other animals, such as goats and sheep.

RIVER CITY

Most of the year, Cairo is hot and dry. Summer lasts for about eight months. The hottest months are June, July, and August. However, winter evenings can get cold. And, central heating does not exist in Cairo. Sandstorms blow in the spring.

Cairo only receives about one inch (3 cm) of rain per year. So, the Nile River has always been important to the Cairenes. This river's main source is Lake Victoria in Uganda. In the past, rains often swelled the river farther north in Egypt. When these floodwaters lowered, rich **silt** was left behind.

Ancient celebrations once centered around the Nile River. Cairo celebrated flooding with parades of decorated boats. But, if the floodwaters did not reach a certain level, the celebrations were canceled. Instead, people prayed and **fasted**.

This Nilometer dates back to when the pharaohs ruled. Nilometers were used to measure the Nile River's water level.

The Nile no longer floods. In 1970, the Aswan High Dam was completed 500 miles (805 km) south of Cairo. The dam controls the floodwaters by releasing the water when needed.

Because of this flood control, farmlands near the Nile River no longer receive the rich **silt**. So, agricultural production has decreased.

Construction on the Aswan High Dam began in 1960.

CAIRENES

Most Egyptians consider themselves Arabs. Arabic is Egypt's official language. About 90 percent of Egypt's population is Muslim. **Islam** is the state religion. To the Egyptians, Islam is more than a belief system. It is a code of conduct.

In Cairo, there are more than 1,000 mosques. Five times a day, the call to prayer rings out to the Cairenes. Many of the festivals that are celebrated in Cairo come from Islam.

Most of Egypt's Christian population is **Coptic** Christian. The northeast portion of Cairo is home to most of the city's Copts. In this area, churches dot the landscape.

In Cairo, religion shapes the family unit. Muslim tradition states that the husband must support his wife and family. Marriage is seen as a legal contract between families rather than individuals. Women have little choice over whom they marry. And, it is very important for children to respect their parents.

Opposite Page: The Rosetta Stone was discovered in 1799. It contains hieroglyphic text as well as the Greek translation.

HIEROGLYPHICS

An ancient form of Egyptian communication is hieroglyphics. These pictures represent sounds and ideas. It is Egypt's oldest form of writing, dating back to about 3100 BC.

Egyptians used hieroglyphics for about 3,500 years. When they began using the Greek alphabet, the meanings behind the pictures were forgotten.

When the Rosetta Stone was discovered, hieroglyphic translation became a possibility. Scholars and historians were able to slowly piece together the meaning of the various hieroglyphics. Much of our knowledge of ancient Egyptians has come from the translation of these pictures.

An important part of family life is dining together. Many Egyptian dishes are not native to Egypt, they are shared with their Middle Eastern neighbors. A typical Egyptian breakfast consists of bread and cheese. Sometimes olives or fried eggs are served, too.

In Cairo, lunch is the main meal. It is eaten later in the afternoon, when the men and children are back home. Stewed vegetables, such as chickpeas or fava beans, are popular.

Not many Cairenes eat out at restaurants. However those who do, eat late. Restaurants don't usually fill up until nine or ten in the evening. It is not unusual to see families dining at one or two in the morning!

Arabic calligraphy and religion are taught at the primary education level.

Just as eating together in Cairo is important, so is education. Primary education in Cairo is required. Children ages 6 to 14 must attend school. Despite overcrowded classrooms, 58 percent of Egypt's adults can read and write.

Students are not required to attend college. However, Cairo is the center of Egypt's higher education. It is home to al-Azhar University, the oldest university in the **Islamic** world. More than 100,000 students attend the more modern Cairo University and 'Ain Shams University.

EGYPTIAN STAPLES

There are many foods eaten in Cairo. Fuul *is made from small, brown beans. The beans are soaked overnight and then boiled and mashed. The mixture is then spooned into a pocket of* shammy, *which is pita-like bread.*

Ta' amiyya *is mashed fava beans and spices. These ingredients are then fried in a patty and stuffed into a shammy with salad and sesame seed paste. This is also known as falafel.*

Lamb is the favorite meat in Cairo. It is most commonly used in shish kebabs. Chicken is popular, too. A common dessert is baklava. This is layers of pastry filled with crushed nuts and pistachios and covered with syrup. Baklava is usually served in small, diamond-shaped pieces.

OLD CAIRO

To defend itself from invaders, walls were built around Cairo. The walls and gates are still standing. This section is Old Cairo. **Coptic** churches stand throughout this historic neighborhood. The most famous is called the Hanging Church. It was built between two towers of Babylon.

The Church of St. Sergius also has an interesting location in Old Cairo. It was built on top of a cave. Its location was chosen because it is believed that Jesus Christ and the Virgin Mary settled there. This is based on the story of their journey into Egypt, which is described in the Bible.

The oldest mosque in Old Cairo is the Mosque of 'Amr ibn al-'As. It was founded in AD 641, but it has been destroyed and rebuilt many times. So, nothing remains of the original building.

North of Old Cairo is a section called **Islamic** Cairo. Many of its mosques date back to **medieval** times. They still stand watch within the Citadel.

The Egyptian ruler Saladin built the Citadel in the 1100s. It served as both a fortress and a royal city. Starting in 1176, the Citadel served as a fortress against attacks by the Crusaders.

The Mosque of Muhammad Ali dominates the southern enclosure of the Citadel. Its alabaster walls, domes, and slender minarets are of a Turkish style, which is an unusual sight in Cairo.

PYRAMIDS

Tourists also visit other Cairo attractions. In southwestern Cairo stand the Pyramids of Giza. These pyramids are the oldest of the Seven Wonders of the World. They are also the only wonder remaining. Three pyramids make up the Pyramids of Giza.

The Great Pyramid is the largest. It was originally 481 feet (147 m) tall. But, it is now 30 feet (9 m) shorter after losing some stones. This pyramid was built during King Khufu's reign from 2575 to 2465 BC. The king's tomb rests here. The two smaller pyramids contain his son and his grandson.

An estimated 2.3 million blocks form the Great Pyramid. Workers cut, moved, and assembled the stone. Some blocks weigh as much as nine tons (8 t)! The workers probably built ramps to haul up the blocks. This was an amazing engineering feat.

Opposite Page: Early visitors to the Pyramids were able to climb the Great Pyramid. And, many carved their names into the stone. In the 1980s, scaling the Great Pyramid was banned.

Another wonder stands guard to the south of the Pyramids, the Great Sphinx. This giant statue has the body of a lion and the head of a king wearing his headdress. The Sphinx faces the rising sun. The sandstone statue was once buried in sand, which saved it from disappearing.

Today, the Sphinx is in danger. The modern city of Cairo is creeping closer. Pollution and rising groundwater are the two main threats. But, there is a project in the works to restore and conserve the Sphinx.

King Tutankhamen's death mask

The Egyptian Museum is another popular destination in Cairo. The most captivating exhibit displays the contents of King Tutankhamen's tomb. This **pharaoh** reigned until his death at age 18 in the 1300s BC.

King Tutankhamen's tomb was unearthed in AD 1923. It contained fabulous treasures, including a solid gold death mask. It was found covering the head of the mummy. Golden statues guarded Tutankhamen. They helped the pharaoh on his journey into the afterlife.

MUMMIES

More than 70 million mummies were made in Egypt alone.

Ancient Egyptians believed that death led to eternal life. They hoped that after death, the soul would return to the body. They wanted the body to be well preserved for this. So, they became the masters of mummification.

To start the embalming process, Egyptians removed the body's internal organs. Next, they rinsed the body with wine. Then, they covered and packed the body with a kind of salt and left it to dry.

After 40 days, the body was ready for restoration. The Egyptians massaged the body's skin and stuffed and perfumed it. Then, they painted it. Finally, they coated the body in warm resin and wrapped it in linen.

CELEBRATIONS

Muslims celebrate Ramadan during the ninth month of the **Islamic** year. Ramadan is the Islamic holy month of **fasting**. Muslims believe they are honoring a commandment from God. During this month, nothing is eaten between sunrise and sunset.

On the twenty-seventh night, Muslims pray to angels who bestow blessings. The fast ends when the new moon rises at the beginning of the tenth month. This is celebrated with a feast.

Another festival honors the birthday of El-Hussein, the prophet Muhammad's grandson. Rides, food stalls, and sideshows are set up in the streets. And, snake charmers draw cobras out of baskets!

In addition to festivals, Cairenes also enjoy sports. Across Egypt, soccer is the most popular sport. The first soccer games broadcast on Egyptian television in the early 1960s. Almost overnight, soccer fever gripped the nation. Now, children start kicking soccer balls as soon as they can walk.

The Pyramids of Giza light up during a concert.

GLOSSARY

assassinate - to murder a very important person, usually for political reasons.

Copt - a person descended from the ancient Egyptians.

delta - the area of land at the mouth of a river that is formed by the deposit of sediment, sand, and pebbles.

economy - the way a nation uses its money, goods, and natural resources.

fast - to go without food.

fez - a cone-shaped, flat-topped hat without a brim. It is usually made of red felt and has a tassel.

fundamentalist - a person who supports strict devotion to a set of principles.

Islam - the religion of Muslims. It is based on the teachings of Allah through the prophet Muhammad as they appear in the Koran.

medieval - of or belonging to the Middle Ages (from AD 500 to 1500).

pharaoh - an ancient Egyptian king.

sect - a small group sharing the same beliefs and principles.

silt - fine sand or clay that is carried by water and settles on the land after a flood.

textile - of or having to do with the designing, manufacturing, or producing of woven fabric.

World War I - from 1914 to 1918, fought in Europe. Great Britain, France, Russia, the United States, and their allies were on one side. Germany, Austria-Hungary, and their allies were on the other side.

SAYING IT

Al-Qahirah - awl-KAH-hee-ruh
Fatimid - FAT-uh-muhd
Gamal Abdel Nasser - guh-MAHL AHB-duhl NAH-suhr
Menachem Begin - muh-NAH-kuhm BAY-gihn
Menes - MEE-neez
pharaoh - FEHR-oh
Sphinx - SFIHNKS
Tutankhamen - too-tan-KAHM-uhn

WEB SITES

To learn more about Cairo, visit ABDO Publishing Company on the World Wide Web at **www.abdopub.com**. Web sites about Cairo are featured on our Book Links page. These links are routinely monitored and updated to provide the most current information available.

INDEX